D0593067

To My Mother

Other Titles by Marci
Published by
Blue Mountain Arts®

Friends Forever
A Celebration of Friendship and Everything Friends Share
Through the Years

A Grateful Path
Inspirational Thoughts on Unconditional Love,
Acceptance, and Positive Living

A Sister Always... A Friend Forever
A Celebration of the Love, Support, and Friendship Sisters Share

Copyright © 2007 by Marci.

All rights reserved. No part of this publication may be reproduced, stored in a retrieval system or transmitted in any form or by any means, electronic, mechanical, photocopying, recording or otherwise, without the written permission of the publisher.

Library of Congress Control Number: 2007925745
ISBN: 978-1-59842-251-1

Children of the Inner Light is a registered trademark. Used under license.

◻ and Blue Mountain Press are registered in U.S. Patent and Trademark Office.
Certain trademarks are used under license.

Printed in China.
First Printing: 2007

✪ This book is printed on recycled paper.

This book is printed on fine quality, laid embossed, 80 lb. paper. This paper has been specially produced to be acid free (neutral pH) and contains no groundwood or unbleached pulp. It conforms with all the requirements of the American National Standards Institute, Inc., so as to ensure that this book will last and be enjoyed by future generations.

Blue Mountain Arts, Inc.
P.O. Box 4549, Boulder, Colorado 80306

To My Mother

Your Love Is a
Lasting Treasure

Marci

Blue Mountain Press™
Boulder, Colorado

Introduction

Your mother was the very first person to love you, and that alone makes her special! She opened her heart to your unique spirit as you came into the world. She made a commitment to you and gave you what you needed to become the person you are. Her love is with you always and is one of the treasures in life that lasts forever.

Mothers have so much love to share. Everything they are a part of turns into something great and wonderful. They are always there to answer the call, whether it's a call to love... a call to sacrifice... a call to give and receive... or a call to feel joy and sorrow to the depths of their being.

For the many things you want to thank your mother for... for all the precious memories she has given you... for the sense of family she has provided... and for all the love she has shown you, I hope these words give voice to your deepest feelings, enabling you to say the things to your mother that you have always wanted to say.

May you celebrate the journey you have taken together, sharing triumphs and setbacks, milestones and birthdays, successes and losses, good times and bad, and all the things that bind you together with love.

Marci

To My Mother

I have come to understand and accept that our lives have been brought together for a reason, and for that I am grateful. Your love is what I needed to grow to my fullest potential. Thank you for the person you are. Thank you for your love and caring over the years. You have seen my best and my worst and have loved me. The bond we have found is everlasting.

Time Has Shown
Me the Blessing
in Your Love

Time has brought me a greater understanding of life and a growing appreciation of all you have been to me. As life's plan unfolds and I am gifted with the experience of living, I see you in a new light. I truly know the love you have given and felt over the years, and I am filled with gratitude.

Your Love Is
a Lasting Treasure

You held me as a baby and let me come into your heart… You nurtured me through childhood and taught me the values that would carry me through life. At times, you let me learn from my own mistakes, but you were always there to dry my tears and share my joys.

You Are Not Just My Mother…
You Are My Guide

You must have had so many
dreams for me when I was born,
but you let me have my own
dreams and supported me through
them, too.

You watched me grow and
change each year, always reminding
me to be true to myself in all of
life's challenges.

You gave me opportunities that helped me discover who I am and gave me the tools I would need to succeed.

You reminded me so often that I was truly loved, and these times have given me so many precious little moments to save.

You let me go when I am sure you wanted to hold on, and that gave me confidence to find my place in the world.

You showed me unconditional love… always.

I Appreciate You
More and More Each Day

When I was young, I did not understand all that a mother gives through the years... but as I have grown, I have realized just how much your patience and encouragement have fostered my growth.

You Are My Mother... and Also My Friend

You've been a friend to me
when I needed a friend... You've
been a confidant when I needed
to unburden my worries... You've
been a mentor when I needed to
be shown the way... You've been
a bright light when I needed a
brighter day... You've made my life
so much better just by being you!

I Am Proud to
Call You Mother

Through the years I have told
you how much I love you, but have
I told you how much I appreciate
you and how proud I am to say
that you are my mother?

You are the mother that everyone wants... You are loving and encouraging... You are there with whatever is needed... And you love me no matter what.

You are a quiet, steady, burning light that inspires me to be my best.

You Are Not Just
a Special Mother,
You Are a Special Person

You are someone I look to when I need guidance. You are someone I hold on to when I need support. You are someone I call on when I need help. You put so much love into everything you do. You are my special mother!

Thank You for the Gift of Family

Our families remind us that
life's most precious gifts are free.

Time spent with loved ones
creates lifelong sweet memories.

A Mother Is…

A mother is a guiding force
through the journey of life.

A mother is the one with the
heart that always understands.

A mother is always there through good times and bad.

A mother is a gift provided by a greater plan.

A mother is a teacher, a mentor, a friend.

A mother is the one who will always love you.

As My Mother, You Have Shown Me Love in So Many Ways

Through time, I have learned that there are many ways to say, "I love you," and you have taught me most of them! You have taught me that love is more than what you say… it is also what you do. So…

For all the meals you planned...
for the endless cleaning up... for the
homework you sat through... for the
illnesses you tended... for the holidays
you made special... for the faith you
shared with me... for the sense of
family you provided...

★

...thank you from the bottom of my heart.

I Love you!

In Case I Ever Forget to Tell You...

In today's world, life gets so busy that the days roll by and we realize we have not spoken to the ones we love! I want you to know that you are one of the most important people in my life, and even if we do not speak every day, my best thoughts and love are always with you.

It Is Hard to Find the Words to Let You Know How Much You Mean to Me

I am so thankful for all you have given over the years, but mostly for the special person you are.

It is not just the love and
concern you have shown...
the help given whenever it
was needed... or the model
you have been... It is all those
things wrapped into one and
given with love and a sense
of constancy.

You are one of the greatest
blessings in my life.

A MOTHER'S LOVE
SHINES
EVERY DAY!

A mother's love is everlasting.

A mother's love
is a lifelong blessing.

A mother's love
is a guiding light.

A mother's love is a
gift that we understand
through time.

You've Always Seen
the Best in Me
and Helped Me to See It, Too

You have always believed
in me and seen the "real me"
shining through no matter what
was happening.

You have loved me through
the hard times and beamed
with joy through the best times.

Thank You for the Gift of Life

Through the years, you have comforted and guided me, taught me about the important things in life, and gifted me with the experience of knowing that I can always depend on you.

You Are Always
There for Me

You are always there with whatever I need. You give me hugs to let me know how you feel... You encourage me to do my best... You remind me that having a family is a gift.

You are the person I call when I need to talk, and I know that you will be there sometimes to "just listen." You are the person that I can laugh with about the most important life events.

You have forgiven my mistakes and dried my tears. You have looked at me with pride for my smallest accomplishments. As only a mother can, you have shown me how much you care.

I Treasure
the Memories
You've Given Me

Remember when you sent me off to my first day of school? You had every little detail just right so my beginning would be perfect.

Remember all my birthday celebrations that you planned and the cards and gifts you gave me so I'd be reminded of how much I was loved?

Remember the hugs of encouragement and the tears that were dried along the way?

Remember the struggles we had as I was finding my way in the world and how you let me go even though it was hard?

I remember all those things, and as I look back I feel so loved.

Did You Know That You Are My Mentor?

You taught me so many important things — things that have made the difference between being successful at life and just getting through.

You taught me mostly by example as you quietly and consistently lived your beliefs.

From you I learned to be on time... to be committed... to work hard... to give my best... to love completely... to sacrifice... and no matter what, to trust God.

I have come to the place where I am so appreciative of you... my mother, my mentor, my guide.

May All the Good Things
You Have Brought to My Life
Be Returned to You

When I need a hug, you are always there with open arms.

I'm returning the favor by wrapping my arms around you with my heart.

For All the Little Things You Do...

I want you to know that your thoughtfulness, your caring, your willingness to please, and all your efforts never go unnoticed.

You've Given Me the Greatest Gift of All

Love

The greatest gift you have given me is the experience of knowing what it means to "love and be loved." You have given so much of yourself through the years, and I am grateful.

My Wishes for You...

I hold in my heart so many wishes for you... I wish you happiness as you begin each day... special love to warm your heart... and tender memories to store away.

I wish that you have peace in your soul as you begin each day with gratitude.

I wish that you know how much I appreciate the mother you are to me and remember that I love you this day and every day.

For the many kind words you have spoken, for the thoughtful things you have done, for the way you are always there sharing the special person you are...

♥

...Your kind and generous spirit shines brightly. You've made such a difference in my life.

Thank You for…

Many moments and days of love.

Opening your heart to me.

Time... a precious gift.

Home... a place to be loved.

Everlasting memories.

Remembering to say, "I love you."

I Love You So Much!

I am so happy to have you in my life. The joys we have shared and the memories we have made through our lives are gifts beyond measure. Your love is a gift I cherish and appreciate more every day. Thank you for being you! I love you!

About Marci

Marci began her career by hand-painting floral designs on clothing. No one was more surprised than she was when one day, in a single burst of inspiration and a completely new and different art style, her delightful characters sprang from her pen! "Their wild and crazy hair is a sign of strength," she thought, "and their crooked little smiles are endearing." She quickly identified the charming characters as Mother, Daughter, Sister, Father, Son, Friend, and so on, until all the people and places in life were filled. Then, with her own loved ones in mind, she wrote a true and special sentiment to each one. This would be the beginning of a wonderful success story, which today still finds Marci writing each and every one of her verses in this same personal way.

Marci is a self-taught artist who has always enjoyed writing and art. She grew up working in her family's small grocery and sub shop. It was there, as she watched her dad interact with customers, she learned that relationships in the workplace and community, as well as in the family, provide the greatest satisfaction and joy.

She went on to develop a business from her home, making home-baked breads, cakes, and pastries to be sold in her dad's store. Later, she started another small home-based business hand-painting clothing for women. At first, she didn't have any idea she could paint and was amazed at how many people loved her work! She was gratified that she could create "wearables" that brought so much joy to those who wore them.

Now as she looks back, Marci sees how all her interests were pieces of a puzzle that fit together and gave her the skills she needed for her work today as artist and author. She is thrilled to see how her delightful characters and universal messages of love have touched the hearts and lives of people everywhere.